Lebensweg:

From the Reich to Rapid City

trillium
memory
books

2016

Printed in the United States of America

First Edition: August 2016

ISBN 978-0-9971549-6-2

Published by
Trillium Memory Books
An imprint of redbat books
La Grande, OR 97850
www.trilliummemorybooks.com

Text set in Palatino and Trajan.

Book design by
Kristin Summers, redbat design | www.redbatdesign.com

~ Table of Contents ~

Richard Heinemann
June 22, 1913 – August 27, 1989

FOREWORD

The following narrative, written in the first person, is the autobiography of my father, Richard Heinemann. As a boy I was fascinated by the stories he would tell about his childhood in Germany, the circumstances of his coming to the United States and the subsequent events in his life. To me, they were as exciting and interesting as any novel. The big difference was that Dad was relating facts, not fiction.

When I became an adult I realized that his life story was worthy of being written down, and would be lost to memory if that were not done. At first, during visits home I would attempt to scribble down some notes as Dad recalled his memories, but it soon became apparent how onerous and inefficient that method was going to be. So instead, I convinced him to make audio recordings of what I hadn't already captured in writing. Then I could transcribe it as time allowed, and replay it as necessary. He gladly did this for me, but it tired him, as his health was failing. His recordings were finished just in time, because he died of cancer on August 27, 1989. It's unfortunate that he didn't live long enough to witness the reunification of East and West Germany a little over a year later, on October 3, 1990. I think it would have pleased him to know that his original homeland was again one nation, which in the Cold War era following World War II had been two separate countries for forty-four years of the seventy-six that he lived.

I said that this is my father's autobiography, and it is, but of course not all of it is word-for-word. In its transcription, I have played the role of editor, to enhance the flow and readability. Dad told me himself that it was difficult to recall the minute details of every event, some of which occurred more than fifty years before the telling. So after a bit of historical research, including consulting public records, in some areas I have added dates or time frames that he wasn't able to provide, and have made minor corrections to some that he did provide. My Tante (Aunt) Inge (Dad's younger sister) provided some of the names and places of their childhood. Still, I was amazed at how little of this type of editing was actually required, and how much detail Dad still remembered.

In other places, again through historical research, I have "fleshed out" some events that he related, but only to give the reader some context and background. For instance, when he described the economic hardships and massive inflation that occurred in Germany during the 1920s, I added in the figures for the rapidly decreasing value of the German Mark, as compared to the dollar. Certain minor corrections were made to some of his facts, not related to his personal experiences, but to the historical record. One example is the event that took place on December 19, 1939. In his audio recording, Dad does not name the ship that intercepted the SS Columbus, but refers to it only as a "Canadian destroyer." That destroyer was the HMS Hyperion, and was in fact British, not Canadian. In no case, however, has it been my intention nor desire to alter the substance of Dad's story, rather merely to enhance it with careful and thoughtful editing.

My hope is that readers in general, and his descendants in particular, will enjoy this retelling of my father's story, and come to appreciate the events that made up his life—the joys, sorrows, hardships, dangers and triumphs. My only regret is how long it took me to accomplish.

Richard T. Heinemann
La Grande, Oregon
May, 2016

• • •

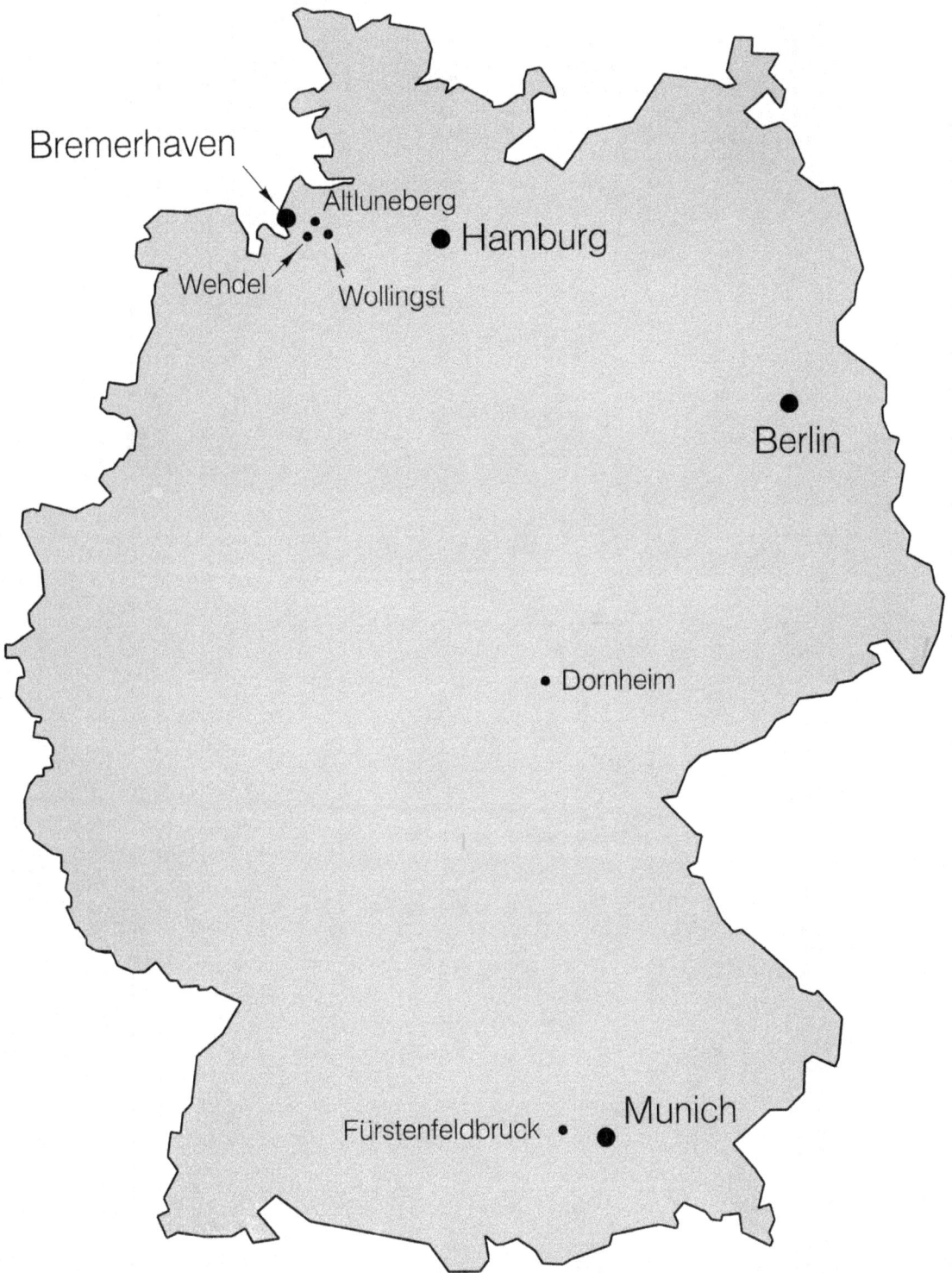

Germany with post-1990 borders and some cities and towns mentioned

1

FAMILY ORIGINS

I was born and raised in northern Germany, in places on or near the North Sea coast. My Heinemann forbears, however, did not originate in that area, so I need to first explain how we came to be there. The ancestral home for many generations was in a forested area of central Germany known as Thuringia. My grandfather, Karl Günther Leopold Heinemann, was a carpenter there, living in the village of Dornheim. After completing his apprenticeship and passing his examination to become a journeyman, he was required by the carpenters' guild (as were all journeymen) to travel for three years around to other parts of Germany looking for work, in order to broaden his experience and improve his skills. Only after that was done might a journeyman be allowed to become a Master Carpenter, with the privilege of owning his own business and hiring other carpenters. In the course of his journeyman travels, my grandfather at one point came to the village of Altluneberg in northern Germany, located a few miles east of what is now the port city of Bremerhaven. He found work replacing the wooden shingles of the church's bell tower. Meanwhile, he made the acquaintance of a local girl named Sophie Ehrichs, and before too long they were married. Then a mandatory three-year stint in the army temporarily interrupted his career, and he was stationed at Hamburg. That's where he settled down with his family after he was discharged from military service.

So that's how the Heinemanns ended up in living in the north of the country. My dad, Wilhelm Eduard Heinemann, was born there (in Altona, now a part of Hamburg). Dad also became a carpenter when he was grown.

As it happened, Dad and Grandpa once went to the town of Wollingst to spend some time building houses for Grandma Sophie's relatives. Wollingst was situated three or four miles south and a little east of Altluneberg. While there, Dad became acquainted with Metta Berthine Bolten, who would later become his wife and my mother. She was the daughter of Claus Hinrich Bolten, who owned what was considered to be a fair-sized farm. My father and mother were married on the 29th of March in 1912, and took up residence back in Hamburg.

Mom had somewhat disappointed her family by marrying "beneath" her farmer/landowner class, into the "common" craftsman/laborer class. The craftsmen and laborers were looked upon as somewhat socially inferior, in spite of being highly skilled, because they owned neither land nor (usually) their own businesses.

• • •

My dad, Wilhelm Eduard Heinemann, as a young man

Mom and me in 1916

2

CHILDHOOD

I was born the oldest of three children on June 22, 1913. About three months later, on the 28th of September, I was christened at St. Johannis Lutheran Church in Hamburg.

Politically, our family leaned toward the Social Democrats. As for religion, we were officially Evangelical Lutherans. Lutheranism was the state religion of Germany, and many Germans were members by default. Dad had grown up as a Baptist, but converted to my mom's Lutheran faith just before they were married, as her family was quite devout.

Sometime after the First World War began, my father was drafted into the army's engineer corps. While he was away, Mother and I went to live with her parents on their farm near Wollingst. It was there in Grandpa Bolten's farm house that my sister Ingeborg was born on January 15, 1915.

One of my earliest fond memories is that of my grandfather, Karl Günter Leopold Heinemann, coming several times to visit us there at the Bolten farm. Whenever he arrived, I would immediately climb onto his lap and search his pockets for candy which always seemed to be there. I believe

My grandpa Claus Hinrich Bolten (Mom's dad)

Grandpa enjoyed the search as much as I did. Sadly, Grandpa Heinemann died on July 6, 1916 in Geestemünde (now part of Bremerhaven).

During the war, my father was involved in the construction of trenches and tunnels at the front. On three separate occasions he was buried alive in cave-ins caused by Allied artillery shelling. As a result, he suffered from debilitating nervous problems, then known as shell shock. (Nowadays it would be called post-traumatic stress disorder, or PTSD.) So, in 1917, he was temporarily released from active duty.

Me, in 1917

Soon after Dad returned home we left Grandpa Bolten's farm, because Dad had acquired a job as custodian of an elementary school in Wulsdorf (also now a part of Bremerhaven). Usually my mother would help him, making it necessary for Inge and me to be there as well. We had to entertain ourselves as best we could around the school yard.

Once or twice a day, Inge and I were sent with two metal pails to get milk and soup from the public soup kitchen, some distance away. The war was depriving many working-class Germans of enough to eat, and this was Germany's version of welfare assistance.

Due to his war injuries, my father would often get relapses of dizziness. He was also very anxious and high-strung. Under these circumstances, I was often severely punished for relatively minor infractions. For instance, whenever my younger sister Inge misbehaved, I was the one punished for it, because I was supposed to be taking care of her.

I remember one incident in particular, when I was playing in the school yard. I suddenly felt the call of nature very strongly. Using the poor judgment of a young boy, I committed the offense of urinating through the fence. For this, my father locked me in the basement of the school for the remainder of the day. To me it was dark and frightening, occupied as it was by scary-looking machinery and cleaning equipment.

When I was four years old and Inge was two, we occasionally played with an older (six years old) neighbor boy named Kalli. He was an ornery, bossy kid, and we were somewhat afraid of him. One day Kalli ordered us, "You two, come over here. We're going to play 'Slaughterhouse'! Richard, lie down there on that bench." At that point, Kalli produced a huge butcher knife, and Inge let out a shriek of mortal terror. Hearing that, Mom came rushing out of the house, pregnant though she was. She grabbed the knife away from Kalli and sent him on his way.

My brother Wilhelm was born on January 30, 1918. About that time my father was required to return to duty in the army, as Germany was losing the war and getting desperate for men to fill the ranks. We had to vacate the school caretaker's quarters, so once again, my mother took us back to live on Grandpa Bolten's farm near Wollingst until the war was over.

Our family in Wehdel. Left to right: Me, Dad, Wilhelm, Mom, Inge

In November of 1918 when the war was over and Dad came home for good, he went to work for Tecklenborg's shipyard in Bremerhaven. We moved to the little town of Wehdel. There was a farmer by the name of Lüder Ronner who owned two large farms, but his family lived on and worked only one of them. On the other place, across the street from the school I attended, stood some outbuildings, stables and storage barns, mostly empty. Also empty was the more recently built house (1908), with ten rooms.

Dad's brother-in-law, my uncle Paul Gebhardt, was a postman for the villages of Wehdel, Geestenseth and Altluneberg. He was able to rent three rooms from Ronner and a kitchen in the big house. Through Uncle Paul's mediation, Dad was also able to rent four rooms in the house. So the Gebhardts— Uncle Paul, Aunt Emma, Grandma Sophie (Ehrichs) Heinemann and little Paul— lived in the back part of the house, while we Heinemanns had the front part. The Gebhardts had a water pump and drain in their kitchen, but we Heinemanns had to fetch water in buckets from a pump outside the house, and carry waste water out in buckets as well.

While living in that house we always had a vegetable garden, and one of my responsibilities was to help maintain it.

Whenever I could, I tried to be helpful to my parents. Once, after my dad had showed me how to split firewood, I took it upon myself to split some for the kitchen stove. The ax hit a knot and glanced off, splitting the big toe of my left foot instead. Mom put my foot into a tub of warm water and iodine, and then sent for the doctor in Geestenseth. In spite of the pain I didn't cry, because I was so fascinated by the spurting blood. While we waited for the doctor, Mom changed the water at least twice. When the doctor arrived, he sewed up my toe without the benefit of any anesthetic. As he was leaving, I remember how amused we children were when he had to push his motor bike, running alongside it, and hopping aboard when the engine started.

I remember another mishap as well. The barn on this property contained an old storage tank set in the floor, which had once been used to collect the runoff of urine and manure from dairy cows. The collected waste would then have been spread on the fields as fertilizer. This particular tank was about half full, perhaps six feet deep. Since the tank had not been in active use for quite some time, its contents had concentrated into a thicker, sludge-like consistency. Around the interior of the tank was a narrow wooden cat-walk. On that day, I was curious to find out just how deep the sludge really was, so I found a long stick with which to probe its depths. I don't know whether I slipped, or if the catwalk collapsed, but I suddenly found my-self submerged over my head in that disgusting stuff. As I went under, my whole life, as the saying goes, passed before my eyes. After a few seconds that seemed like an eternity, I surfaced and was able to breathe again. Some-how I was able to dog-paddle to the edge and clamber out of the tank. Meanwhile, Inge, who was with me when this mishap occurred, had run screaming to Mom and Dad.

As I emerged from the barn, frightened and badly shaken, I heard my father's angry voice. Fearing the severe punishment that was certain to follow for getting myself into such a predicament, I ran away across the pasture, but to no avail. Dad caught me, marched me back home, put me into a wash tub, and scrubbed me with a stiff-bristled brush.

When the bath was finished, my skin was red and raw. Finally, adding in-sult to injury, I was forced to go and find a hazel stick for my own spanking.

One might get the impression that my dad was a harsh disciplinarian. At times he was, but that aspect was far outweighed by the obvious love he had for his children. Just as often, he would be compassionate, and both our parents lavished us with affection. I can say unequivocally that we had a close and loving home life.

In the aftermath of the First World War, the economy of Germany, unlike that of most of the rest of the world, was in shambles. In 1920, 1921 and 1922, the value of the Mark began to fall drastically, and the result was runaway inflation. Previously valued at four Marks to the dollar, by the summer of 1921 it was 75 to the dollar, and a year later in 1922 it was 400. By the beginning of 1923 it was 7000 per dollar. During January of 1923 the Mark fell to 18,000. By the first of July it had dropped to 160,000 and by August to a million. By November it took four billion Marks to buy a dollar, and thereafter the figures became trillions. German currency had become utterly worthless. The life savings of the middle and working classes were wiped out. Cartoons of the time depicted Germans with wheelbarrows of money, in line to buy a single loaf of bread. It wasn't until the last half of the decade that the economy began to stabilize somewhat.

Fortunately, my dad was usually able to find work, in spite of the dismal economic conditions. It was common for working-class laborers and crafts-men in the surrounding villages and countryside to go into Bremerhaven to find work. Dad had jobs at various shipyards (Tecklenborg's, for instance) doing carpentry work on the ships or for the shipyards themselves. At one point, I know he was involved in building the lock for the Kaiserschleuse drydock. When Tecklenborg's shipyard shut down, he signed on as ship's carpenter for a coal freighter that made regular runs hauling coal from Nar-vik, in northern Norway, to Bremerhaven.

In 1922 Dad got a job on another freighter that was about to make a trip to the far east. That time, he was away from home for three years. While he was gone, my mother apparently didn't feel comfortable trying to raise all three of her children without a man around. So at Grandpa Bolten's urg-ing, she arranged with her cousin in the village of Appeln to get me a job working and living on the farm of the Hülsberg family. There I learned to plant potatoes, cabbage and other vegetables behind the plow. I also milked cows, whose milk I transported to the separator in cans loaded on a cart that was pulled by a dog. I bundled and bound shocks of barley, rye and oats. I helped load hay and straw in the fields onto wagons, and from the wagons into the hayloft in the barn. Other jobs included herding sheep or gathering eggs (which I considered fun, because I enjoyed the challenge of finding the hidden clutches in the barn).

In short, my duties involved almost every aspect of farm work. As pay, I ate well and was clothed. It was a hard three years (nine to twelve years of age) and some would consider it little more than child slave labor, but I gained lots of experience and respect for hard work.

When my dad returned home from the sea in 1925 and learned that Mom had sent me away to strangers instead of caring for me herself, he was furious. He wasted no time in fetching me back home.

There were times when Dad worked away from home in other parts of Germany, so sometimes while he was away we would all go temporarily to stay and help out on the farm of my Uncle Louis and Aunt Dora Schumacher (Mom's sister). For me, going there was as good as Christmas, because we always ate so well.

When we lived there in Wehdel the church we attended was in Altluneberg, about a mile and a half away. This was the same church where Grandpa Heinemann had repaired the bell tower roof when he first came to northern Germany as a journeyman carpenter. On April 14, 1927, the Thursday before Easter (Maundy Thursday), the church service was held there during which my Lutheran confirmation took place.

• • •

The church in Altluneberg, built in 1632. Note the wooden shingles on the bell tower. Inge Heinemann in foreground (1993).

3

EARLY ADULTHOOD

Throughout Europe, it was customary that children were required to attend only eight years of public schooling. From there, families with money could send their boys on to institutes of higher learning. Most others were apprenticed for three or four years to learn a trade. I wanted to follow in the footsteps of my father and grandfather and become a carpenter. Unfortunately, apprenticeships in that trade were hard to come by at the time. Some friends of ours had an uncle named Johann Seebeck who owned a bakery in Wulsdorf and needed an apprentice. They convinced my parents to let me take up that trade. So, I apprenticed three years with Seebeck from April of 1927 to April of 1930, and then worked for him as a regular employee for awhile longer.

But business was slow, and I was laid off. The economy of the entire world was in depression during the 1930s, but Germany was even worse off, because the economy had never fully recovered after the First World War. Germany had only about half as much time as other countries to enjoy the prosperity of the 1920s.

It seemed my only option was to go into the Arbeitsdienst, which was a type of government make-work, similar to the Civilian Conservation Corps in the United States at the time. Those of us in the Arbeitsdienst lived in camps, and the crew I belonged to built irrigation canals, roads, and drainage ditches in the peat moors of northern Germany.

About this same time, my dad was employed on a construction project that extended the Berlin subway system.

Adolf Hitler's Nazi Party came to power in 1933. If anything at all positive can be said about a man that would later inflict such evil and suffering upon the world, it would have to be that his policies (or those of his underlings) revitalized the economy of Germany for a little while.

In 1934 my crew was assigned to digging heather sod for the purpose of camouflaging underground airplane hangars. The area where we worked was entirely enclosed by a twelve-feet-high chain link fence topped by barbed wire. All around us were SS guards, which gave one a feeling of being in prison. We were forbidden to tell anyone about what was going on inside the fence. The penalty for disobeying those instructions would no doubt have been actual imprisonment in a concentration camp. I had the common sense to keep silent about the particulars of my job.

That same year my father hired me to come work with him. He had become superintendent of an airport project south of Berlin, under contract to the Butzer Construction Company. On that job I learned the ironworkers' trade, and for the first time in my life Dad and I became close friends. We worked quite amicably together.

Our next project was in Oberschlesian (Upper Silesia), which at the time was in southeastern Germany, but is now a part of Poland. We were building a hydroelectric power dam on the Oder River. Again, as an ironworker, I installed reinforcement bar around which concrete was to be poured.

Then one day my construction career was brought to an abrupt halt by a serious accident on the job. I fell thirty feet through the network of reinforcement bar into the turbine area below. For three days I lay unconscious in the hospital at Opeln. I had suffered numerous injuries, but the worst was to my left knee. After a period of recuperation I found that I was no longer able to perform my duties. Not only was I limited by my injured knee, but I would become dizzy and disoriented by the heights.

I was released from employment at the dam site and returned home to Wehdel. I was hospitalized again in Bremerhaven for additional treatment to my knees, which were still somewhat swollen. After about a month in the hospital I was discharged and immediately reported to the Employment Office. Jobs were still somewhat scarce, since Hitler's employment schemes were just getting started. Having been injured as well, I had little hope for my chances of getting a job. I probably could have found a position helping to build the Autobahn (Germany's freeway system), but that would have required being away from home for extended periods, something I was not yet prepared to do.

My brother Wilhelm was employed as a farmhand for the Gerken family, just across the street from where we lived in Wehdel. Sister Inge was working in the household of a family who owned a fishing fleet.

Bremerhaven was a major fishing port for Europe. The fleet would arrive at the docks in late afternoon or evening and be unloaded overnight. Early the next morning, the catch was auctioned off in big boxes to fish mongers and dealers who had gathered from all over the continent.

I got lucky and landed a job at a plant where herring was packed. It was hard, stinky work. The procedure was to place a layer of fish in the bottom of a wooden barrel, cover it with a layer of salt, then another layer of fish, another layer of salt, and so on, alternating layers until the barrel was full and ready to be sealed. The workers wore rubber aprons and heavy old jackets as protection against the cold and damp. Being saturated with a fishy odor, these items were left hanging in a locker at the end of the day.

Since I had no transportation to and from Wehdel where my parents lived, I rented a room there in Bremerhaven from friends of the family. The first thing I did after work each day was to soak in the bathtub for about an hour, then douse myself with lots of cologne in an attempt to mask the fishy aroma. It did little good though, as the smell of fish had permeated every pore. People who worked in the fishing and fish processing industry were easily identified by the distinct "air" about them.

• • •

4

GOING TO SEA
(FIRST SHIP, SS SIERRA CORDOBA)

I worked there at the herring plant from the latter part of 1934 until March of 1935. Meanwhile, I had submitted an application to the North German Lloyd company for a job aboard one of their passenger ships. In March they informed me of a position opening on one of their smaller ships, the Sierra Cordoba, which regularly made trips to Norway under the Kraft Durch Freude program.

Some explanation is in order here of what Kraft Durch Freude was. Tied down by the control of wages that were barely above subsistence level, German workers were provided by the government with entertainment to divert their attention from the restrictive conditions of everyday life. Dr. Ley (the Nazi Labor Front leader) came up with this organization called Kraft Durch Freude (Strength Through Joy). This provided what can only be described as regimented leisure. No organized social, sport or recreational group was allowed to function except under the control and direction of Kraft Durch Freude. To the ordinary German of the Third Reich, this official all-embracing recreational organization was better than nothing at all, since one was not trusted to be left to one's own devices. It provided workers with dirt-cheap vacation trips on land and sea. For example, those in northern Germany might take tours through the Alps or the Black Forest in the south, while people from southern Germany might take a cruise on one of the Kraft Durch Freude ships chartered by Dr. Ley, and home ported in a northern coastal city.

The Sierra Cordoba was one of those chartered ships. As I said, it made trips from Bremerhaven to the fjords along the Norwegian coast. Never did we dock in a Norwegian port, however. Our passengers had to be content with admiring the beautiful coastal mountains, forests and fjords from aboard the ship. Each trip lasted five or six days, after which we would return to Bremerhaven for a couple of days to unload the passengers and pick up another group, then repeat the trip along the same route as the one previous.

• • •

5

ABOARD THE SS COLUMBUS

I worked aboard the Sierra Cordoba until about the end of the second season in 1936, at which time I again received a notice from North German Lloyd, informing me of another job opening as a cook aboard the luxury liner, SS Columbus.

I jumped at this new opportunity, as the Columbus was no Kraft Durch Freude ship, but rather one on which people of wealth from all over the world embarked for cruises in luxury and style.

This magnificent vessel was built by the F. Schichau yards in Danzig, Germany (now Gdansk, Poland) and was christened in 1922. At the time she was first launched, the Columbus was the largest and fastest ship in Germany's passenger fleet. By the time I came aboard, she still ranked third, exceeded only by the SS Europa and the SS Bremen. She was 774 feet long, 83 feet wide and displaced 32,354 gross tonnage. She was capable of traveling at a speed of 23 knots and could accommodate 1650 passengers, plus about 650 crew members. She had one of the first outside swimming pools ever installed on a cruise ship and had a platform for nighttime dancing.

When I reported aboard the Columbus, I was immediately put to work helping to clean every nook and cranny of the food processing department (kitchen, coolers, etc.), and to restock supplies in preparation for our next cruise to New York in September of 1936.

One of the first acquaintances I made on board was Paul Müller, one of the two barber and beauty operators. His boss was the other one. Paul was what I considered to be well educated, as he had attended some college before coming aboard the Columbus. Besides German, he was fluent in English and Spanish, which was helpful when interacting with passengers. When I had a break from my work in the food department, usually between noon and 2:00 p.m., Paul would sometimes ask me to come and give him a hand in the beauty salon. I would shampoo the hair of the ladies, which Paul would then set and style. In the evening after my work in the kitchen was done, I would return to help him clean up. When that was finished we would often go out on deck if the weather was good, to talk and enjoy the stars and night breezes. In fact, we sometimes did this in inclement weather as well, just to thrill at the waves crashing onto the decks.

Some of our conversations were about the Bible and the prophesies contained in it. I don't know whether Paul was a devout Christian (I think he was a Presbyterian), but he was interested in that kind of thing, and he was the first person who ever introduced me to that aspect of scripture. He felt that some of the events happening in the world and in Germany's Third Reich might be a fulfillment of some of that prophesy. In retrospect, I wonder if some of our conversations may have been overheard. On board ship, and in fact in every aspect of German life, there were always Nazi party members and SS officers around somewhere, spying on people and monitoring their political views and loyalties. This may have been the first embryo of our falling out of favor with the Nazi sympathizers on board, and of our being "blacklisted," so to speak. At first, they probably weren't too concerned with us, as they were busy pursuing their own plans, intrigues and financial interests. But as time went on, all of that would eventually change for the worse.

In the barbershop and beauty parlor, Paul received most of his tips in American dollars. For helping him, he shared some of his largesse with me. This was always a welcome addition to my supply of dollars. We were only allowed to exchange enough German Marks each month to obtain four

My second ship, the beautiful luxury liner SS Columbus

American dollars. Since the dollar was the strongest, most widely accepted and desired currency worldwide, every crew member took any opportunity they could to obtain more.

Our schedule of cruises typically involved operations in the north Atlantic during the spring and summer months, starting in March or April, and then in the autumn and winter, there were trips to the West Indies and/or around South America. Summertime operations sometimes included Caribbean/West Indies trips as well, but most of those were winter season cruises. I made two trips around South America, one in 1937 and another in 1938. In early 1939 we went around Africa. These continental circumnavigations could take as long as two months. During the Caribbean/West Indies cruises, we would usually visit a different island group each time, and they might include Cuba, Jamaica, Haiti, the Bahamas, Puerto Rico, Aruba, Curaçau and the Antilles. I don't think we ever went to Bermuda, though.

After I first came aboard in 1936 we crossed the Atlantic to New York, and then went on to the Caribbean. We considered New York sort of a "second home port" because all of our autumn and winter season cruises started and ended there, beginning typically around September, the season lasting six or seven months.

In the spring and summer of 1937 and 1938 we made two or three trips between Bremerhaven and New York. We called these "shuttle trips," because they were mostly made to relieve the SS Bremen and the SS Europa of some of the high volume of cross-ocean traffic between the two ports. A number of the passengers were Germans who were financially comfortable, making the trip to visit their emigrant relatives in America. Likewise, many Americans of recent European descent would visit the "homeland" in Germany or other parts of Europe. German-Americans, and German citizens living in America especially, were curious to visit Germany and see just what it was that Hitler was up to. We heard stories in later years of German-American businessmen who had been enticed to return to Germany in the 1930s to invest their money in businesses there. In exchange, they were allowed various privileges, profits and other benefits. Some ended up losing everything they had, and the outbreak of war trapped some of them in Germany. Many who were fortunate enough to survive were unable until war's end to return to the former good life they'd had in the United States.

During these crossings, and particularly in 1938 after Austria was annexed by Germany, Paul came into contact with a number of high ranking wealthy German officials and industrialists. Among these were the heads of companies like Krupp, a major armament manufacturer, Thyssen, a large steel trust, and I.G. Farben, the chemical cartel that was responsible for producing Zyklon B, the poison that was eventually used in the death by gassing of millions of Jews and other concentration camp inmates. These companies all had holdings in the United States and other countries, as well as in Germany. There was also the former Crown Prince Friedrich Wilhelm, son of the exiled Kaiser Wilhelm II. Such influential and powerful men were all in Hitler's good graces for one reason or another. Either they had contributed financially to the Nazi party, or had lent their position and influence in Hitler's rise to power.

In Paul's job, he was often in a position to overhear the conversations of these men. They discussed business or pleasure amongst themselves, and with businessmen of other nationalities. Being a friend and confidant, Paul would naturally relate to me much of what he overheard in the barbershop.

We both felt it was hypocritical that these Germans of power and influence should be on such amiable terms with so many foreigners. After all, the propaganda of the Nazi party was constantly reminding us that we should hate and despise the "inferior" British, French and Americans. Again, in retrospect, I suspect the ever-present "ears" were eavesdropping on us and were aware of our doubts concerning the credibility of the regime. As time went on, it became obvious that our rendering of the mandatory greeting of "Heil Hitler" was only half-hearted. It no doubt pushed us closer to the status of "undesirables."

Besides these summertime "shuttle trips" there were also three trips from New York to Norway, with a stop on the way at Halifax, Nova Scotia. These cruises were similar to the ones I made on the Sierra Cordoba, with one big difference. The Columbus passengers were mostly well-to-do, and of course were allowed to go ashore at various ports of call, as was the crew. The west coast of Norway is indented by incredibly beautiful fjords, with picturesque cities and towns. We visited Stavangerfjord, Hardangerfjord, Bergen, Sognefjord, Trondheim and Narvik. Narvik was a major iron ore loading port in northern Norway, above the Arctic Circle. The fjords are an awesome sight, with forested mountainsides and rocky cliffs rising in places almost straight up from the water's edge. When the crew had a chance to go ashore, the experience was enhanced by the fact that many of the locals spoke German as well as their native Norwegian, making interactions with them more enjoyable.

After completing these trips to Norway we returned to Bremerhaven to clean the ship and restock supplies in preparation for going to New York, our base for the winter cruise season.

The winter cruise season usually included eight to ten trips to the West Indies with, as I mentioned earlier, one longer trip per year around South America or Africa. I learned some Spanish on the South America and West Indies cruises, but forgot most of it in later years, especially when I started to learn English.

After each trip we returned to New York for a few days of time off and to prepare for the next one. Going back and forth repeatedly between the warmer southern latitudes and the colder weather in New York could be a shock to the system, which I didn't particularly enjoy. Prior to departure

On the streets of New York

from New York and again on our return, I was often prevailed upon by the ship's stewards to help carry luggage for the passengers. For this extra bit of work the stewards paid me a few dollars, which I welcomed. Doing this, I saved enough to buy several tailor-made suits on Third Avenue, as well as other clothing, Leica binoculars, a camera, some bedding and suitcases. These types of things were difficult to obtain in Germany, due to rationing. I was always planning ahead for the future, so some of these items I would turn over to my parents at home for safekeeping. If I ever got married, at least I'd have something to start with. Unfortunately, certain things I kept with me were lost when the ship was scuttled. But more on that later.

As early as 1937, I had begun tossing around the idea of becoming an American citizen. I was impressed by the lifestyle of freedom and by the opportunity the strength of the economy seemed to offer. When I discussed this idea with my parents, my mom was all for it. My dad, while not opposed, was more circumspect. Little did I realize that another twelve years would pass before my dream of American citizenship finally came to fruition.

• • •

6

AROUND SOUTH AMERICA

Acruise around South America of course involved transiting through the Caribbean. We stopped at Havana, Cuba, and then continued on to the Panama Canal. Anyone who has ever passed through that canal on a ship was probably as impressed as I was. It is an amazing feat of engineering. About forty-eight miles long, by a system of locks, it raises a ship eighty-five feet over the spine of the isthmus of Panama from one ocean to the other. The trip takes several hours to complete. In general terms, the Atlantic/Caribbean side lies to the east and the Pacific side to the west. However, what's interesting is that due to the S-shaped curve of the isthmus, the canal runs from the northwest on the Atlantic side to the southeast on the Pacific side, almost the opposite of what one might think. The highest point of the transit is at Lake Gatun, an enormous reservoir created by the damming of the Chagres River when the canal was built. The dam has hydroelectric generators that produce the electricity for operating the canal system. From Gatun Lake you pass through the Culebra Cut before entering the locks that lower the vessel back down to sea level on the Pacific side.

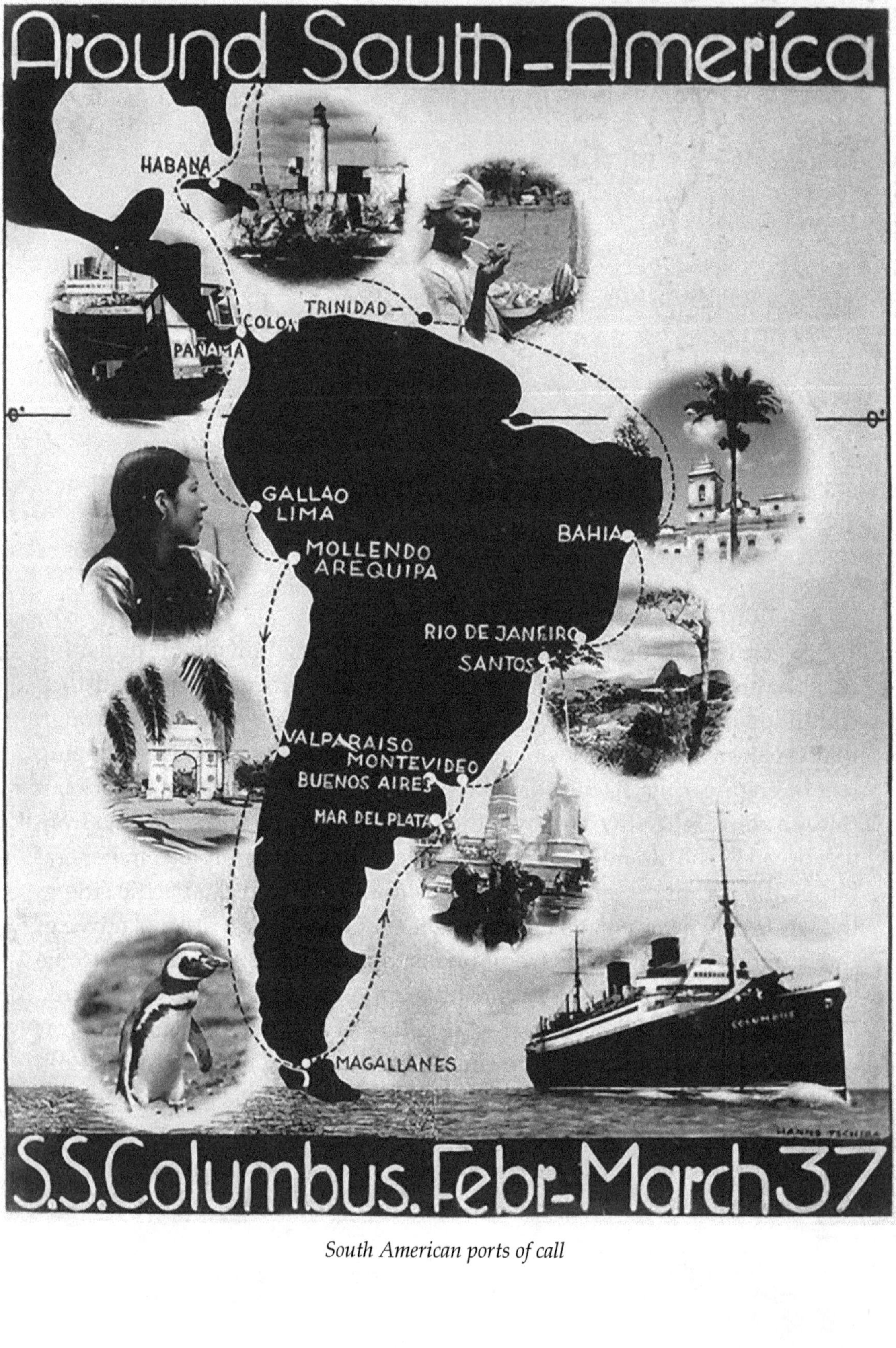

South American ports of call

From Panama we sailed south down the Pacific coast of South America. For most of the way the majestic Andes Mountains were visible in the distance, averaging about thirteen thousand feet above sea level, but with a few peaks that rise above twenty-two thousand feet. In at least one of the ports, we weren't able to tie right up to the pier, but had to anchor offshore. The passengers would be ferried back and forth to shore in the ship's motor boats, of which I think we had about seven.

In Peru we stopped at Callao, which served as the port area for the capitol city of Lima, a few miles inland. Another Peruvian port was Mollendo, with the city of Arequipa being inland from there.

The next stop was at Valparaiso, Chile. Some of the passengers decided to disembark and take a train over the Andes Mountains to Mar del Plata in Argentina, spending time there while the ship, with the remainder of the passengers still aboard, continued south around the southern tip of South America through the Strait of Magellan (with a brief stop at Magallenes, the city now called Punta Arenas), and back north up the east coast of Argentina. Mar del Plata was a resort town and a playground for the rich and famous. I think some of the passengers may also have visited Buenos Aires while they had the time. From Mar del Plata we crossed the large delta to the next port of call, which was Montevideo, Uruguay. The crew wasn't allowed to go ashore there, because we only stayed in port for one day.

Then it was on to Santos and Rio de Janeiro, both in Brazil. Approaching Rio de Janeiro, you're treated to a view of the majestic thirteen hundred foot Sugarloaf Mountain, situated at the mouth of Guanabara Bay, on a peninsula that juts out into the Atlantic Ocean. The pier where we docked was right in town. While the passengers enjoyed themselves in the city and on its lovely beaches, and took bus tours to surrounding areas, we crew members had time to go ashore as well. Some of us rode the cog-wheel railway to the top of Corcovado Mountain, where the one hundred foot statue of Christ the Redeemer overlooks the city. As impressive a city as Rio de Janeiro was, it also had its seedy side. There were squalid shanty towns with dirt-poor beggars and street vendors, as was the case in almost every city.

In some ports of call (including some in the West Indies), there were natives who would swim out to the ship where we were anchored offshore, yelling for passengers to throw coins into the water. Then they would dive down and retrieve the sinking coins. That was how they made their living. Others would come alongside in small boats loaded with tropical fruits, woven basketry or beautiful local art work to sell. At first most of the passengers enjoyed and were amused by all this. Eventually however, the novelty wore off and some of the passengers began to consider it a nuisance, not wishing to be pestered quite so often. Consequently the ship's officers started limiting access of these boats and swimmers, demanding that they keep their distance.

After departing Rio de Janeiro we had one more stop to make in Brazil, which was the port city of Bahia. Nowadays this city is known as Salvador, or Salvador de Bahia.

Our last stop on the South American cruise was at the island of Trinidad, which is the larger of the two main islands that make up the nation of Trindad and Tobago, off the northeast coast of Venezuela. From Trinidad then, we returned to New York.

• • •

7

AROUND AFRICA

On February 4, 1939, we got underway from New York for a cruise around Africa. The transit across the Atlantic took about seven days, during which we passed within view of the Azores, but didn't stop there.

The first port visit was at Casablanca in Morocco. To me, it was a strange and exotic place, inhabited by Berbers and Arabic-speaking people. In the public marketplace, the women pretty much kept to themselves and were shrouded from head to foot in cloth. When a stranger walked by, a part of the wrap was drawn across the face so that only the eyes were visible. The men, on the other hand, would swarm around like vultures, always wanting to sell you something. If you didn't know what you were doing, you could end up losing all of your money. Even so, items like goat leather or camel leather were a good bargain.

From Casablanca, the next stop was at the port of Santa Cruz on the island of Teneriffe in the Canary Islands. Next was Dakar, Senegal, the western-most point on the coast of Africa. A few days later we were in Jamestown on the island of Saint Helena, where Napoleon Bonaparte was exiled from 1815 to 1821.

Next on the itinerary was the nation of South Africa at the southern tip of the continent, with stops at Cape Town, Port Elizabeth and Durban. The countryside is beautiful, and Table Mountain, with its flat top, forms a dramatic backdrop to the city of Cape Town. Most of the locals spoke Afrikaans, a language with its roots in the Dutch spoken by the first European settlers. We encountered a number of locals who could speak German as well, which helped with our understanding and enjoyment of the area when we went ashore.

Continuing north up the east coast included a visit to Andoany (formerly Hellville) on Nossi Be (a small island just off the coast of the larger island of Madagascar), then on to Zanzibar in Tanganyika (now Tanzania) and Mombasa, Kenya.

Rounding the eastern Horn of Africa, we transited the Gulf of Aden and passed through the Bab el Mandeb Strait into the Red Sea. The oppressive heat there was unforgettable.

I should pause here to explain that at many of our ports of call, passengers usually had the opportunity to take additional side trips or tours to points of interest farther inland, or else to locations farther up or down the coast from the city where the ship was moored. In the Red Sea we stopped briefly at Port Sudan (in Sudan), just long enough to disembark passengers who were participating in one of those additional excursions.

Arriving at the city of Suez in Egypt, we began our transit through the Suez Canal to Port Said, our last stop in Africa. I have never seen such a barren landscape as the sandy wastes on both sides of the Suez Canal. The wind was blowing and filled every nook and cranny of the ship with fine-grained sand and dust, and irritated our eyes with the grit. We closed all the portholes to keep it from invading the ship's interior, but with limited success.

Departing Port Said, we left Africa behind, sailing east and north through the Mediterranean Sea to Naples, on the west coast of Italy. The volcano, Mount Vesuvius, is clearly visible from Naples, and while we were there, smoke was erupting from its summit. We crew members only had the opportunity to go ashore into the city of Naples itself, but the passengers were able to make a day trip to Pompeii if they wished. There was even time for some of them to go as far as Rome.

African ports of call

From Naples we proceeded northwest to Villefranche, on the French Riviera. This port is right next door to Nice, and only about six miles or so from Monte Carlo, across the border in the Principality of Monaco. The Casino in Monte Carlo has long been a gambling mecca for tourists, and it goes without saying that some of our passengers availed themselves of the opportunity to lose some money there.

The last stop on this cruise was Gibraltar, a British territory on the Strait of Gibraltar, which is the western entrance to the Mediterranean. From Gibraltar we crossed the Atlantic back to New York to drop off the passengers and end the cruise in April of 1939.

• • •

8

LAST MONTHS OF THE SS COLUMBUS

As soon as the passengers from the Africa cruise had been disembarked in New York, we returned to Bremerhaven and the ship went into dry dock for several weeks to get refurbished. In June we headed back to New York for a season of cruises from there. This was earlier than our normal winter season that usually started in September, the reason being that we were scheduled for a long, round-the-world cruise later on. First, however, we were supposed to fit in a few of the customary West Indies cruises.

Beginning what I think was to be the last of these scheduled West Indies cruises, we got underway from New York on August 19, 1939. From news stories and radio dispatches, we were aware of the rising political tensions in Europe between Germany and some of the neighboring countries. In the backs of our minds we were wondering what, if anything, might eventually transpire.

On August 22nd we anchored off St. Thomas in the Virgin Islands. This was a normal enough one-day port visit, with the passengers being shuttled by boat to shore and back. The next day, however, when we arrived at St. Pierre on Martinique, the French police allowed our passengers to go ashore, but not the crew.

From there we sailed to Bridgetown on Barbados for a brief stay, and then continued west to Willemstad on Curacao. When we arrived at Willemstad, there was disturbing news that events in Europe seemed about to boil over, and that war might be imminent. Nobody was allowed ashore, not even the passengers, who were understandably upset. It was also the case that from then on, our orders would be coming directly from the German Naval High Command, rather than from the North German Lloyd company.

Knowing that we would probably soon be ordered home to Germany, Captain Dähne decided it was time to cut things short and head for New York to unload the passengers. So we got underway on August 30th, headed north. The same day we received orders to offload all the passengers in Havana, Cuba, so that's what we did instead. On September 1st Germany invaded Poland.

We left Havana on the second of September, steaming full speed for Veracruz, Mexico. Previous orders had instructed us to put into a neutral or friendly nation's port, and wait there for further orders. Our captain had determined that Veracruz was the best place to do that. We dropped anchor in the harbor there on September 3rd, the same day that Britain and France declared war on Germany, followed within a few days by British Commonwealth nations like Australia, Canada, New Zealand and South Africa. World War II had begun.

Our stay at Veracruz would end up lasting for three and a half months. During that time all of the non-German crew members were removed and turned over to their consulates. They included the Chinese laundry workers, and I believe some Italians. We were anchored quite a long distance offshore. Those of us who were not in the good graces of the Nazis were only allowed to go ashore about once a month. The officers and Nazi party members, on the other hand, went ashore much more often. I can't say for certain, but I strongly suspect that in addition to their own money, they may have been squandering the ship's funds as well. In any case, supplies eventually ran low. We didn't get enough fruits and vegetables, and some of the crew even suffered from scurvy, a malady that one usually associates only with mariners of past centuries.

Many countries had consulates in Veracruz, including some which were now at war with Germany. Naturally, they kept close tabs on any German vessels in the harbor vicinity. They knew when each one arrived, what its activities were, and when it departed, and would relay that information to their respective governments or allies. Their intention was to intercept and capture any German vessel, civilian or military, that attempted to transit international waters. Not only would the Columbus be a great prize to capture, but it was in the interest of Britain and her allies to prevent any German men of military age from returning home where they could be added to the fighting forces.

Finally, we received orders to leave Veracruz and try running the blockade in hopes of making it home to Germany. If that were unsuccessful, and we were in danger of being captured, the ship was to be scuttled to prevent its falling into enemy hands. The planned route was to hug the coast of the United States for as long as possible, then head northeast on a northern circuit past Greenland, Iceland and northern Norway, then south to Germany.

In anticipation of the worst case scenario, a special scuttling team had been trained and repeatedly drilled on how to go about quickly and efficiently conducting the destruction and sinking of the ship. In conjunction, the rest of the crew was constantly drilled on the procedures for manning the life boats and abandoning ship.

We got underway on December 14, 1939. Immediately, we were shadowed by two destroyers of the United States Navy, the USS Benham and the USS Lang. Being neutral and not yet at war, the United States had extended its normal three mile territorial waters to include a three hundred mile "neutrality zone," meant to enhance and defend that status. To enforce it, U.S. Navy ships, as part of the Neutrality Patrol, would monitor the zone and any vessels of the nations at war with one another, to prevent any belligerent actions by them within that zone.

In our transit around Florida and up the east coast of the United States, the U.S. Navy destroyers that were shadowing us would from time to time be relieved and replaced by others. There were at least eight different ships involved, and maybe more, performing this duty in groups of two or three at a time. Besides the Benham and the Lang, there were the USS Jouett, USS Schenck, USS Philip, USS Ellis and USS Cole. These "escorts" had to report their positions at least every eight hours, and maybe even more often. This was done over open radio transmissions. Consequently, any British or Allied ship could monitor these position reports and thereby know exactly where the Columbus was located.

Early on Monday, December 18th, when we were approximately 250 miles off the coast of North Carolina or Virginia, we noticed that our American destroyer escorts had suddenly been relieved by a much larger 10,000 ton heavy cruiser, the USS Tuscaloosa. We wondered at the reason for this exchange. Maybe the Tuscaloosa was supposed to accompany us on the last leg before we left the neutrality zone. Apparently the Americans knew something we did not.

• • •

9

SCUTTLED

On the morning of Tuesday the 19th we left the neutrality zone and broke out into international waters. The events of this day would turn out to be a disaster for our beautiful ship, but for some of us crew members who were anti-Nazi, it was also a blessing in disguise. We found out later that this was the day we were to have been confined in the ship's empty fuel bunkers. That would have been disastrous for us, probably fatal.

At about 3:00 in the afternoon a warship suddenly appeared from starboard, approaching at a high rate of speed. It was the British destroyer, HMS Hyperion. As she came nearer, she sent a flag signal ordering us to stop, and then fired a warning shot across our bow. Escape was impossible, so at the sound of an alarm our crew rushed to our abandon ship stations and began to man the boats.

In the space of about ten minutes, most of us were in the boats (seven motor boats and about twenty lifeboats propelled by oars). Meanwhile, the scuttling team had gone into action. They opened all the seacocks to let seawater in, then spread flammable liquids throughout the ship and set it on fire, before finally heading for the boats themselves. As we made our way towards the Tuscaloosa a couple miles distant, some of the lifeboats

The SS Columbus on fire. Note the HMS Hyperion on the horizon.
The men in the lifeboat (foreground) are not identified. COURTESY JAMES MCBRIDE

were fortunate to be towed in groups by the motorboats, while in others, the occupants had to put their backs into pulling hard on the oars. The sea was getting rougher, which made progress toward our goal more difficult. Finally, the scuttling crew, and last of all Captain Dähne, were able to leave the ship and join our flotilla of boats. It was getting dark, and the Columbus, now fully engulfed in flames, lit up the sky and the surrounding sea behind us. The sound of an occasional explosion from within the Columbus punctuated the eerie scene.

While all of this was going on, some interesting radio traffic had begun between the Hyperion and the Tuscaloosa. The Hyperion's captain sent a message, saying he wanted to take fifty or sixty Columbus prisoners, including the captain and officers. The Tuscaloosa replied with, "Our orders are that either you take them all, or we take them all," knowing full well that the

Hyperion had no room to accommodate all 579 of us. The Hyperion's captain, no doubt angry at being forced to give in to such an ultimatum, began to maneuver his ship in and out amongst our boats in an attempt to swamp us with a combination of the wake and an already turbulent sea. Seeing this, the Tuscaloosa radioed a stern warning to the Hyperion, ordering her captain to stop harassing our lifeboats, or else be fired upon. Fortunately, the Hyperion complied and steamed away from us.

Around 4:00 our boats at long last started arriving alongside the Tuscaloosa, and her crew lowered Jacobs ladders and cargo nets so we could climb aboard. The ordeal was not yet over, however. Grasping a rung of the ladder required perfect timing, so that when a swell raised the boat to its highest point, you could make a grab for it before the receding wave dropped the boat out from under. Often, more than one attempt was necessary to succeed. Some missed or lost their grasp, fell into the water, and had to be rescued. Others were injured when they did manage to hang on, because when the boat returned on the next rising swell, it slammed the crew member against the Tuscaloosa's hull.

Finally, by 5:00 p.m. we had all made it aboard the Tuscaloosa and stood on the deck shivering with cold and weariness, so exhausted that we could barely keep our eyes open. Forlorn and wet, we were nevertheless glad to have been rescued by the Americans, rather than having been taken prisoner by the British. We watched numbly as our once proud luxury liner, aflame from stem to stern in the distance, slowly settled deeper into the ocean. Sadly, we learned later that night that two of our fellow crew members had in fact not made it off the ship alive. I heard that they had probably been asleep after a long watch, and upon hearing the alarm to abandon ship, had ignored it, thinking it was just another bothersome drill. So 577 of us had survived. Finally, the Tuscaloosa turned away from the scene and steamed toward New York.

Soon we were taken below to the mess decks and fed. The supper menu for the Tuscaloosa's crew that night had included chicken fricassee. We were impressed when they graciously forfeited their own intended meal so that we would have something substantial to eat. They themselves made do with sandwiches. Besides the fricassee, we had all the vegetables and drinks we wanted. Given the circumstances, that was probably the best meal I had ever eaten.

The Hyperion sent a final message to the Tuscaloosa, informing her that the Columbus had sunk to the bottom of the ocean at a little after 11:00 p.m. on December 19, 1939, at latitude 38 degrees, two minutes North and longitude sixty-five degrees, thirty-three minutes West.

A bit of irony in this whole incident was that the Tuscaloosa's captain, Harry Badt, was a Jew. He was surely aware of the poor treatment Jews were enduring in Germany's Third Reich. Yet for the entire time we were aboard his vessel, we were treated with the greatest respect. Maybe that was driven in part by official policy or by his orders. But it seems to me that his kindness and compassion went well beyond what those orders would have required.

• • •

10

ELLIS ISLAND

The next day, December 20, 1939, the Tuscaloosa arrived at New York, and late in the afternoon pulled up to a berth in Staten Island. All of us Columbus survivors were put on motor launches and transferred to the Ellis Island immigration station where we were processed by having our names and other information about us recorded. Next they assigned us sleeping quarters with cots. There weren't enough cots, however, and some of the crew had to sleep on the floor. It was very crowded, as the immigration station had not been prepared for such a large influx.

A pall of uncertainty hung over us, because we didn't know what our status was, or what was going to happen to us next. For the time being, we were classified as "distressed seamen." The German government and the North German Lloyd company wanted to have us returned to Germany as soon as possible, so they began negotiations with American Immigration Service and State Department officials to get that accomplished. Sending us home across the Atlantic was not a viable option, due to Britain's stated intention not to allow any Germans of military age to return to Germany. As our experience had already shown, they were patrolling the Atlantic, and attempting to blockade the German coast as well. Fifty or sixty of our crew consisted of women, boys under seventeen years old and men over fifty-two years old, so the British did eventually allow those to return home on an Italian ship.

Meanwhile, since accommodations at Ellis Island were strained beyond capacity by our presence, they wanted to find somewhere else to put us. One proposal was put forth to move us to various YMCA facilities around the New York area. That idea was rejected by our German officials, who felt it was important to keep us all together.

We celebrated Christmas on Ellis Island with a traditional American Christmas dinner, and were allowed to have visitors. I had called my Uncle John Bolten who lived in Brooklyn, one of the boroughs of New York City. He and his family had emigrated to New York from Germany in May of 1927. Ironically, the ship on which they themselves had arrived at Ellis Island was the SS Columbus. Uncle John (Johann, in German), Aunt Gesine and cousins Anni and Henry came to visit me a few times. They bought some clothing items for me that I badly needed, like trousers, shirts, shoes and additional toiletries, since all I had were a few personal items that I had been able to quickly stuff into a bag when we abandoned ship. These visits from the Boltens and from friends I had made in the last couple of years were an enormous boost to my morale.

The days stretched into weeks, and finally we heard that an agreement had been reached whereby we would be transported by rail across the United States to the west coast. Then we were to board a Japanese ship bound for Japan. From Japan we would go to the Russian port of Vladivostok, board a train to cross Russian Siberia and eastern Europe, and eventually end up back in Germany.

On January 14, 1940, just over five hundred of us boarded two trains in Jersey City, New Jersey for the four or five day cross-country trip to San Francisco, California. Our route took us through Chicago, Illinois to Omaha, Nebraska and Laramie, Wyoming, then on to Ogden, Utah and Reno, Nevada and over the Sierra Nevada Mountains to Oakland and San Francisco.

At Reno our trains were met by the German Consul General of San Francisco, Fritz Wiedemann. His consular post had been awarded to him by Hitler, who favored him because he had been one of Hitler's superior officers (a captain) during the First World War, when Hitler was only a corporal. At that time, Wiedemann had been supportive of Hitler, and was well liked by him.

Wiedemann had come to tell us of the arrangements he had made for a Japanese freighter that was to take us to Japan. He went on to report that by the time we arrived at our destination, that ship would already have left port, because of news that Allied warships were waiting offshore. The Japanese steamship company didn't want to risk taking us on board, only to be stopped and have us seized by those warships. As it turned out, other incidents had already occurred in which Australian and Canadian naval ships had stopped and boarded merchant vessels to remove any German nationals. Apparently not only the Atlantic, but the Pacific as well was now being patrolled. The German government didn't want to risk losing more than five hundred able-bodied seamen who could be used to fight for the German Fatherland. Consequently, the plans for sending us home were put on hold for the time being. For some of us, this news was a great relief.

• • •

11

ANGEL ISLAND

When we arrived in San Francisco on January 18, we were immediately loaded onto a ferry boat and transported to Angel Island in San Francisco Bay to await further developments.

Angel Island is one of the larger islands in San Francisco Bay, situated about a mile and a half or a mile and three quarters north of Alcatraz Island. At the time, the major installations on Angel Island were the Quarantine Station located on the northwest side of the island at Ayala Cove, the Immigration Station on the northeast side at China Cove, and Fort McDowell, an army base on the east side. Fort McDowell functioned as the Overseas Discharge and Replacement Depot for the west coast.

About two thirds of the crew, myself included, were housed at the Quarantine Station. I worked in the big dining hall there, where we fed the crew. The rest of the crew, including Paul Müller, were housed at the Immigration Station. Paul volunteered to run the laundry there.

When we had the time, some of my friends and I would walk over to the Immigration Station to visit with Paul, or to help him in the laundry. We were pretty much allowed to go anywhere on the island we wanted, except for Fort McDowell, which was off limits. However, once in a while small groups of us were allowed to visit the canteen there to buy things like ice cream or cigarettes.

In February the U.S. Immigration Service changed the crew's status from "distressed seamen" to "excluded aliens." Technically, our movements were supposed to be more restricted and more closely monitored. Shore leave off the island was limited to about twenty-five or thirty people a day. That meant that a normal opportunity to get off the island only came around about once every three weeks or so. But there were always some of the crew who weren't interested in going, and their passes were available for others of us to use. So I ended up going ashore quite often and had a wonderful time. There were new friends and acquaintances to be made among the German community in the Bay area. One of these was a German woman who ran a grocery store in Daly City. I got to know some of her friends as well. She showed us around the attractions of San Francisco and surrounding areas, like the Presidio, the cable cars, Golden Gate Park, the redwood groves at Muir Woods, and the sea lions on the coast. All of this diversion helped somewhat to temporarily dispel the dark clouds of uncertainty hanging over me.

During times when we had to remain on the island, a half dozen or so of us who were close friends would often just hang out together and talk. Paul Müller, of course, was one of us. Our conversations were mostly just general in nature, and not really directed against the Nazi regime or the Party. Still, those ever-present "ears" seemed to always be somewhere nearby, just waiting to catch some snippet that could be construed as disloyal.

As time went on, conditions and events developed that were pushing the German and American officials toward a decision to move us to somewhere other than Angel Island. First, repeated attempts to find ways to get us back to Germany had failed. On different occasions, they had tried to ship out a few dozen or so of our more "elderly" crew members over fifty-two years old, on Italian or Japanese freighters, thinking the Allied nations would let them through. But in every instance, the freighter was stopped by a warship and the Germans removed. Second, even when we had first arrived, the Immigration officials had been reluctant to accommodate such a large number of us on Angel Island for more than a couple of weeks. To make matters worse, a fire broke out at the Immigration Station Administration Building where some of the crew were lodged, and it burned down. Those crew members had to be moved over to the Quarantine Station with us, making conditions even more crowded. Thirdly, tensions were on the rise between the United States and Japan, which was on friendly terms with Germany. The scenario began to seem more feasible in which the U.S. might somehow become involved in the war. American public opinion and sentiment was also becoming less favorable toward Germany, and having us located near the coast was now viewed as a security risk. The American government decided it was time to move us to a more secluded location farther inland, with enough room to accommodate the 410 of us crew members that still remained on Angel Island.

• • •

12

FORT STANTON

During the latter part of 1940 the Immigration Service, accompanied by our Captain Dähne, began looking for a suitable place to relocate us. After several weeks of searching, they found what seemed to be an adequate facility. Dähne returned to Angel Island in January of 1941 and reported that we were to be transferred to a Civilian Conservation Corps (CCC) camp in New Mexico, called Fort Stanton. The camp would be turned over to the Immigration Service, and our internment there was to be administered by the Border Patrol.

The camp still needed some work done on it before it was ready for us to occupy, so in January, thirty-eight or thirty-nine of our crew were sent ahead to help with that. They built additional barracks, a kitchen and mess hall, and toilets and showers. They converted a couple of the smaller existing buildings into a medical dispensary and quarters for the Border Patrol officers. In February another group of about forty was sent to supplement the first one. Paul Müller was in one of those two advance contingents.

On March 15, 1941 the rest of us were put on a train in San Francisco, and we arrived at the station in Carizozo, New Mexico on the 17th. From there we rode Greyhound busses the rest of the way to Fort Stanton.

My bunk in the barracks at Fort Stanton

Fort Stanton was situated at over 6200 feet in elevation on the arid high desert between two mountain ranges, the Capitan Mountains to the east and the Sierra Blanca (White Mountains) to the west. The nearest town was the little village of Capitan, about three or four miles to the northwest. The city of Ruidoso was ten or twelve miles southwest of the camp. The camp was bordered on one side by the Rio Bonito, a little stream that was dry for most of the year, except during the spring snowmelt in the White Mountains, or when heavy thunderstorms passed through. Then it would become a raging torrent. Directly across the Rio Bonito from the camp was a merchant marine hospital for tuberculosis patients, run by the Public Health Service.

Having been one of the cooks on the Columbus, I of course worked in the camp's mess hall. Paul Müller volunteered to run the laundry again, as he had at Angel Island. And again, five or six of my close friends and I sometimes went over and helped him. The laundry was a T-shaped building. In one wing was a boiler for heating the water, as well as the washing ma-

I helped out in the laundry at Fort Stanton. I'm the one with rolled up trousers and sleeveless shirt.
COURTESY JAMES MCBRIDE

chines and a couple of large mangles for pressing bed linens. Clothing items like shirts had to be ironed by hand. In another part of the building were numbered cubby holes, each one assigned to a crew member, where each man could come to retrieve his own clean laundry.

In addition to regularly assigned duties, most of the crew were involved on a voluntary basis in work to improve our living conditions and beautify our surroundings. Soon after we arrived, one of the first things we did was to build a swimming pool, which had to be dug out by hand. The concrete and most of the other building materials were provided by the U.S. Government. That project took two or three months to complete. After that, a sports field and tennis court were built, and more buildings were constructed along with additions to some of the existing ones. All the buildings, both existing and new ones, were painted to make them more attractive. We installed rock and cactus gardens using drought-resistant plants we had dug up from the surrounding countryside. We also planted some colorful flower beds. Foot paths were laid out and bordered with rocks or brick. Besides enhancing the camp's livability, all of these projects helped to keep us busy and improve morale by taking our minds off our situation.

For the first nine months or so of our internment at Fort Stanton, we had a lot of freedom during our time off to come and go as we pleased. We'd hike to the nearby town of Capitan or go exploring in the area. We'd stroll for miles along the dry creek bed of the Rio Bonito. Occasionally we'd run across small abandoned buildings which we'd been given permission to dismantle. We salvaged the lumber and brought it back to camp so we could build our own little private huts to spend free time in.

In December of 1941 everything changed when the United States became involved in the war. On December 7th, the Japanese bombed Pearl Harbor, and the next day both the U.S. and Britain declared war on Japan. On the 11th, in support of Japan, both Hitler and Mussolini (the Italian dictator) declared war on the U.S., which immediately reciprocated with its own declaration. So now America was an ally of Britain, France and the Commonwealth nations in the war against Germany, Italy and Japan. Our official status at Fort Stanton had suddenly changed from "excluded aliens" to "enemy aliens."

Almost immediately, the Immigration Service began building a high fence around the camp, with guard towers and flood lights. As civilians, we were technically "internees," not prisoners of war. But the result was the same. Our freedom to move beyond the confines of the camp was gone and a nightly curfew was established. Being that we were civilians, a sort of informal "gentlemen's agreement" or understanding came about that, while the Border Patrol would of course be in charge of security and general administration of the camp, the day-to-day activities, work assignments and discipline would be left to Captain Dähne and the officers, just as if we had been aboard ship. Fort Stanton held the distinction of being the very first internment camp established in the United States during World War II.

One of the camp's buildings contained a small short-wave radio setup that the ship's officers had considered important enough to rescue when the

Columbus was scuttled, as well as a few other items, like the ship's cash and manifests. Our small group of friends included a radio operator whose job it was to receive broadcasts from Germany about what was happening at home, particularly how the war was going. There might be information such as major victories or setbacks for Germany, how many casualties, how much enemy armament was destroyed, etc. This information was then relayed to the crew at the daily 6:00 p.m. gathering at the canteen, which everyone was expected to attend. If the news was good, then there would be jubilation among the Nazi Party members and their sympathizers.

On some days the radio reception was poor, either garbled or nonexistent. Yet our radioman friend was still supposed to provide something for the evening gathering. On those days he might come to us and say, "I don't have anything to report. What am I gonna do?" So we would sit around and make up something for the day's report, like such-and-such a campaign was successful, or so many planes were shot down or this many tanks were destroyed, and so on. When that happened, we weren't particularly interested in standing around at the daily news gathering, listening to a litany of our own lies. As often as not, we simply "forgot" to attend. These absences were noticed by the Nazi Party members and ship's officers. No doubt this resulted in a further accumulation of black marks against us.

They were always aware of our general lack of enthusiasm for the Nazi regime. We weren't openly rebellious or even critical, but small things like declining to join the Nazi Party, or that we participated only reluctantly in activities expected of a loyal citizen of the Third Reich were duly noted. I believe that regular reports were somehow conveyed back to Germany, because we were often told, "When we get back to Germany, you're going to hang from the nearest lamp post." That was always the threat. Sometimes they insulted us with insinuations of being homosexual.

In early February of 1942 the whole camp started coming down with trichinosis. Trichinosis is a parasitic disease caused by eating undercooked meat (usually pork) that contains the larvae of the trichinella roundworm encased in a cyst. Your stomach acids dissolve the cyst, releasing the larvae, which burrow into the intestinal wall and mature. They produce more larvae that get into the bloodstream, and eventually into the muscle tissue, where they themselves become encased. While all of this is going on, the body's immune response causes diarrhea alternating with constipation, cramps, vomiting, fever, headache, swollen glands, puffy eyes, dizziness, muscle pain and fatigue. The symptoms can last for three or four weeks.

This trichinosis outbreak was caused by infected pork that we got in food supplies from one of the towns nearby. Most of us weren't aware that American meat inspection regulations weren't nearly as stringent or thorough as they were in Germany, even though our butchers had warned Captain Dähne and the ship's doctor that the meat should be inspected. In Germany trichinosis was practically unknown, because the law required (and still does) that every butchered animal carcass be carefully inspected or tested so that no infected meat reaches the consumer. This rule applied not only to commercial butchers, but even to any animal that was slaughtered by a farmer for his own use. In fact, in Germany we were so comfortable with the safety of our meat that one of the things we liked to eat was Mett, a sort of pâté made of raw ground pork and beef with an egg and seasoning mixed in, and then spread on our dark rye bread or pumpernickel.

Not everyone got sick at the same time. It started out with thirty or forty men, then a couple days later another group got sick, then another bunch, and so on. The outbreak lasted probably two or three months. Our group of five or six weren't affected until near the end. While many others were suffering and we ourselves were still relatively healthy, we had to do laundry every day because there were large volumes of clothing and bedding that was soiled and smelly from diarrhea and vomit. We erected makeshift latrines near every barracks, but it didn't help much to reduce the volume of laundry. We even visited some of the sick men and assisted the medical staff and orderlies from the tuberculosis hospital in taking care of them. Those that had so recently labeled us as traitors were now suddenly as meek as children, grateful and more than happy to have us looking after them. But when almost everyone else was getting better and we ourselves were ill, they began to get cocky again and reverted back to their former ways. Their attitudes toward us were lacking the same compassion we had shown to them.

As 1942 progressed, the war for Germany wasn't going as well as previously. There were setbacks in Russia and North Africa, and the Allies had started heavily bombing German cities. So now it was evident there was a real possibility of Germany being defeated. Tensions between our group and the Nazi faction steadily increased, as did the level of their threats against us. They began telling us, "If Germany loses the war, you won't have the chance to blackmail us. We'll kill you first".

In early November (I think it was on the 5th or 6th) some of the Nazis apparently had decided it was time to make good on their threats. Paul Müller had befriended one of the Border Patrol guards, an older man we called "Pop." His duties involved patrolling the perimeter of the camp on horseback as well as occasionally manning one of the guard towers. On this particular day there was a creepy, ominous air in the camp, like the calm before a storm. That morning, Paul was chatting with Pop, who said something to the effect of, "It's too quiet. Something's wrong." Paul agreed, and replied that he thought something bad was going to happen that day. Pop informed him that later on he'd be stationed in the guard tower nearest the laundry, and if something should start, Paul was to give him a signal.

Sure enough, around 4:30 or 5:00 in the afternoon, about a dozen or so of the Nazi thugs rushed into one of the barracks where some of our friends were living. As soon as we noticed this, Paul gave a signal to Pop in the tower, who immediately called for help. Four or five Border Patrol officers entered the camp and rushed to the barracks where the trouble was. Unfortunately, because of the previously mentioned "gentlemen's agreement," these officers were unarmed. So the thugs simply grabbed them and shoved them into a narrow locker area near the entrance of the barracks, where they could be easily confined by a few men. The others started beating up on our friends. Their intention was to hunt down anyone in camp who wasn't openly a Nazi sympathizer, and give them the same treatment. According to their previous threats, however, some of us were in for a worse fate than just a beating. Namely, death.

Meanwhile, a bunch of us ran to the laundry and barricaded ourselves inside, knowing we were the next intended victims. Four windows, high on the walls of the laundry building, were each guarded by one man with a baseball bat or an iron bar. At the junction where the two wings of the T-shaped building converged was a door. The door consisted of an outer storm door, inside of which was a heavier main door, which we had barricaded with a two-by-four board. Paul was positioned just inside this door with a five gallon can of gasoline. I was a short distance away with a large iron bar inserted into the boiler's fire. Our plan of defense was that if our attackers should manage to breach the reinforced door, then I was to hand my red-hot iron bar to Paul, and he would thrust it into his can of gasoline. The result, we hoped, would be an explosion that killed the attackers, but almost certainly ourselves as well. This would no doubt be an act of suicide, but if we were to die anyway, better to take them with us and deprive them their satisfaction of having killed us.

It wasn't long before the Nazi mob discovered where we were, and started battering the door to get at us. It was difficult for them to break through, but eventually the door began to splinter, on the verge of giving way. I was just about to hand my red-hot iron bar to Paul when we heard shots outside. Additional Border Patrol guards had entered the camp, this time armed with weapons and tear gas. The shots had been warning shots, and then they set off the tear gas canisters. They herded the entire crew, except for those of us in the laundry, into the fenced sports field and locked the gate. Then they came over to the laundry and let us out. We were ordered, along with about thirty or so others who were also identified as being anti-Nazi, to pack our bags. We were loaded into trucks and driven to El Paso, Texas for temporary safekeeping. They put us up in the very large immigration station there, which was basically an annex of the El Paso County jail. That was the first and last time ever for me in a jail cell.

• • •

13

FORT LINCOLN, PAROLE AND RELEASE

After three days spent in the El Paso County jail, we were shipped to Fort Lincoln in North Dakota, another internment camp. We arrived there on November 11, 1942.

Fort Lincoln was located five miles south of Bismarck on the east side of the Missouri River. It had been a former military post that was converted to an internment camp in April of 1941, shortly after Fort Stanton. It housed other Germans who had been merchant seaman before the war, as well as Americans of German descent who were considered a security threat. One usually only hears about the Japanese-Americans that were unjustly interned during the war, and what a black mark on America's history that was. But it's a little-known fact that some American citizens of German or Italian ancestry were interned as well.

There were some pro-Nazis in Fort Lincoln who were inclined to start the same kind of problems we'd experienced at Fort Stanton. Fortunately, the Immigration Service already had their number, and shipped them away to Fort Stanton before they could cause any trouble, where they would be with others of their own ilk.

I was assigned to work in the hospital kitchen, and got paid for it.

A few months after I arrived at Fort Lincoln, a number of the internees, myself included, requested and were granted a parole hearing, which for me took place in April of 1943. At the hearing I was placed under oath and interviewed by the parole board. I expressed my desire to remain in the United States and become an American citizen as soon as I was allowed. I also said that I would volunteer to serve in the United States military. My reasoning was that if I was to make this country my new home, I had to be willing to fight for it. My application was unanimously approved by the board, and I was one of forty-four internees which were in the first group to be paroled on July 7, 1943.

My group of parolees was released to the Northern Pacific Railroad to work on its Extra Gang #4. Our job was to repair the section of track that ran all the way from Mandan, North Dakota eastward to Fargo and across the Red River to Moorhead, Minnesota. We also built some spur lines where a freight train could pull off the main track to allow a higher priority troop train to pass. I enjoyed working outdoors, but being light-skinned, I also suffered a lot that summer from repeated sunburns and the heat given off by the creosote-impregnated railroad ties.

I happened to make the acquaintance of a regular railroad employee by the name of Josiah (Joe) Long. He worked at the siding in Dawson, and his job was to replenish the steam locomotives with coal and water. Little did I know that about a year later, Joe would become my brother-in-law. It so happened that he was the half-brother of my future wife Mabel, whom as yet I hadn't even met.

In so many places I had been, it seemed I had encountered at least a few people who spoke German, either because they were from Germany, or were of German descent. This was especially true in North Dakota, because so many of them had settled in the Dakotas during the previous fifty or sixty years. Even the boss and foreman of our extra gang spoke German.

I worked on the railroad until November of 1943. Our last project was to build a "Y" of track that allowed a locomotive to pull off the main line and turn around to go in the opposite direction. When that was finished we were assigned a new parole officer. Soon after, we were released in Fargo from Immigration Service jurisdiction altogether, and were now free agents.

Some of those released found other work across the river in Moorhead, but most stayed in the Fargo area. I got a job at White's Café in West Fargo near the stockyards, working as a fry cook. There again, I met a lot of German-speaking customers, most of them truck drivers. I enjoyed my job, but the difficulty for me was not knowing much English. Sometimes I got confused when the waitresses would yell in the orders fast and furious. Fortunately, one of the waitresses, Erna Müller, was a German Jew who had come to the United States in 1937 or 1938 to escape persecution in Germany. Whenever I had trouble understanding the waitresses, I'd ask Erna in German, "Erna, was haben die gesagt?" (Erna, what did they say?) I was forced very quickly to acquire a working knowledge of English, and Erna was a big help in that regard.

In January of 1944 I quit my job at White's Café to take another one working evenings at Time's Café, which was across the street from the Northern Pacific railway station in Fargo. It was owned by a Greek family.

Time's Café was where I met Mabel Long. She was waitressing there for a couple of hours in the evening while attending business school during the day. In addition to her pay she was allowed one meal.

There was a kitchen helper and salad girl who spoke a little German. One day she approached Mabel and said, "Mabel, why don't you invite Richard to go on a bicycle ride with us?" Being a little shy, Mabel replied, "Well, why don't *you* ask him?" So after a couple days of back-and-forth like that, I finally got the invitation. We rented three bicycles and rode from Fargo to West Fargo and back, stopping by the café to chat with some of our fellow employees. We had a great time, but Mabel found it hard to understand me. As time went on though, my English improved.

• • •

14

ARMY INDUCTION
AND MARRIAGE

In June of 1944 I finally got the call to report to Fort Snelling, near Minneapolis, Minnesota for induction into the Army. After being sworn in on June 19, 1944, I was immediately sent to Buckley Field, a base near Denver, Colorado, for boot camp (basic recruit training).

As I began my training, my left knee started bothering me so much that I wasn't able to march or drill. This was the same knee that had been injured in an accident while working on a dam construction project in Germany. After a medical examination they admitted me to the base hospital and performed surgery to remove some bone fragments and pieces of cartilage.

While I was in the hospital, Mabel came all the way from Fargo to visit me. I told myself that if she thought enough of me to do that, then I had better marry her. She agreed.

On August 12, 1944 I received a one-day furlough from the hospital to get married. We went into Denver, and on crutches I climbed the twenty-five steps of the courthouse, where we obtained our marriage license. Then we returned to the base chapel for our wedding ceremony. A fellow patient in the hospital bed next to mine stood in as my best man. His name was Bernie Gussoff. His wife Esther was Mabel's matron of honor, and the two of them were also our witnesses. After the ceremony, a group of about six of us went back to downtown Denver for a wedding dinner. I only had the one night off and had to report back to the hospital the next morning. So that was how Mabel and I began our married life together.

At the beginning of 1945 I got out of the hospital and had to repeat some of the training I had missed, but was excused from the more strenuous aspects of marching and drilling.

After completion of basic training there was the not uncommon period of waiting around for assignment to a permanent duty station. Just to keep us busy and give us something to do in the meantime, the new soldiers were set to picking up cigarette butts day after day, along with a lot of other mundane "busy work."

Meanwhile, Mabel and I lived in a one-room apartment, which was basically just a living room with an adjacent tiny closet-sized room that had been converted into a kitchen. Space was so tight that when I was in the kitchen cooking, there was no room for Mabel to move past me or even be there at the same time.

• • •

Our Wedding Day, August 12, 1944

15

BERKELEY AND CARMEL

Finally I received orders assigning me to the 411ᵗʰ Army Air Forces Base Unit (AAFBU) headquarters in Berkeley, California. At the time, the Air Force was still a part of the U.S. Army. It wasn't until a couple years later that Congress made it a separate military branch, the U.S. Air Force.

Being sent to Berkeley was kind of a pleasant surprise for me, because being in the San Francisco Bay area, I was back where I had been five years earlier while on Angel Island. Now I would have the opportunity to reconnect with friends I'd made back then.

Available housing was scarce in the Bay area because so many people from all over the country had come there to work in the war industries, like the shipyards in Oakland and Richmond. Luckily, we were able to find a place to share with another family. We had one small room for our own use, but both families used the same kitchen.

Eventually I bought a house trailer, which I think was sixteen or eighteen feet long. To us it was a huge blessing, but nowadays, even camping trailers are bigger than that. I built a ten-by-ten addition onto it to give us a little more room. Mabel's sister came and stayed with us for awhile, and slept in the living room on the couch. That made space kind of tight, but she had a daytime job, so at least it was only in the evenings that things were crowded.

Around the same time I also bought a car, a 1939 Lincoln Zephyr two-seater coupe with a twelve-cylinder engine. That purchase turned out not to be much of a bargain though, because on a trip to Arizona later on, the main bearings went out and I couldn't find a replacement crankshaft.

For extra income I did some janitorial and maintenance work in the trailer court. Mabel got work as a waitress right there in El Cerrito, the little town where we lived.

Our first child, a boy, was born in the Berkeley hospital on September 1, 1945. We named him William Richard, but called him simply "Willy."

That autumn the 411th transferred me to their Point Sur radar installation, located right on the coast about ten or fifteen miles south of Carmel-by-the-Sea. When we first moved down there we set up our trailer in a park just outside of town. Later, a doctor who had a house closer to the radar compound allowed us to park our trailer in his back yard under the trees. That was a lot more convenient for me to get back and forth to work.

I worked in the mess hall. Mabel would drop me off, and then as often as not, she'd just stay around, not really having anywhere else to go. A friend of mine that worked in the radar tower had a wife in the same situation, so the two women would usually sit in the dining hall and talk. Sometimes they'd wander down to the ocean, right outside a few steps away, and watch the waves crash up onto the rocks.

The war by that time was pretty much over, since Germany had surrendered in May of 1945 and Japan had surrendered on September 2nd. The United States no longer needed quite as many military men, so a lot of them were being discharged, based on a point system. Our staff at Point Sur was reduced to such an extent that eventually all that were left were the First Sergeant, a couple of radar operators and I. Cooking for just these few, there wasn't much for me to do.

In April of 1946 my first enlistment ended as well, so I was brought back to headquarters in Berkeley, where I intended to reenlist. At that point I had a

Berkeley, California

decision to make. One option was to take over running the mess hall there at headquarters, which would mean an immediate promotion from my current rank of Sergeant (E-4) to Staff Sergeant (E-5). Headquarters staff, however, thought it a good idea for me to transfer to Germany as an interpreter for the Allied post-war occupation forces. That too would mean a promotion, but not right away. I would first have to acquire my 320 rating (interpreter's qualification). Ultimately I decided on the transfer to Germany, since that would give me the chance to visit my parents, whom I hadn't seen since 1939.

I left for Germany in July of 1946, departing from New York on a troop ship. Mabel and Willy wouldn't be joining me in Germany for several months yet. We drove cross country towing the trailer, and stopped at Carrington, North Dakota to visit Mabel's parents. From there we continued on to Pekin, Illinois where Mabel's sister and brother-in-law, Velda and Herman Maseman, lived. Mabel and Willy would stay with the Masemans until they could join me in Germany.

In Pekin we sold both the trailer and the car, and then I continued by train to New York.

• • •

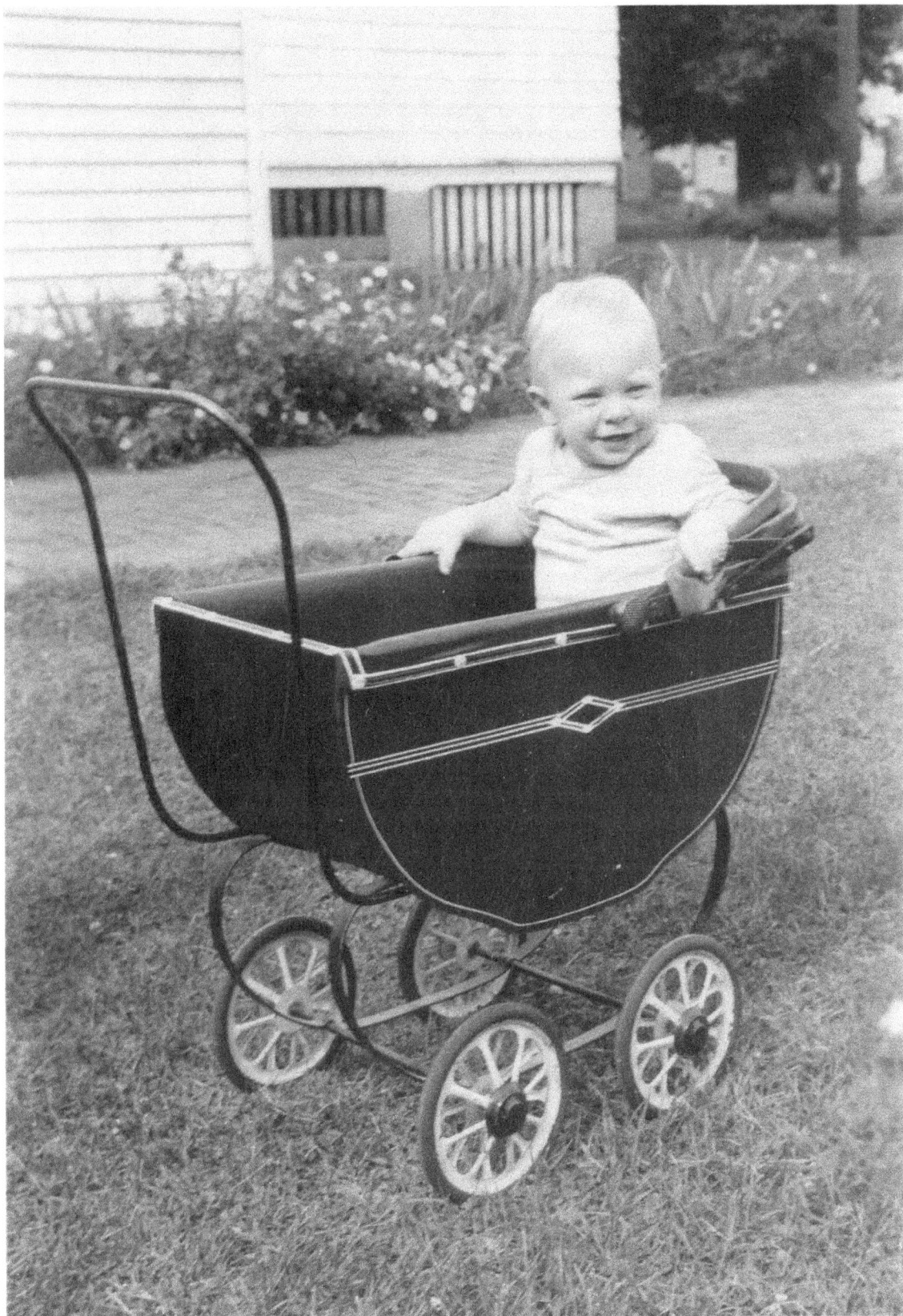

Willy at Herman and Velda's house in Pekin, Illinois

16

FÜRSTENFELDBRUCK

My duty station in Germany was to be the base at Fürstenfeldbruck, a town about fifteen miles west of Munich in southern Bavaria. My point of arrival, however, was in Bremerhaven. Except for the port facilities which the Allies had spared for their own use, Bremerhaven had been heavily bombed during the war, and most of the city was destroyed. I didn't know what to expect when I got there. In fact, as I found out later, a bomb had landed right in my parents' back yard, but failed to explode. A bomb squad came in later to defuse and remove it. Mom, Dad and Inge had come so close to annihilation!

When the troop ship docked in Bremerhaven on August 1, 1946 I knew I was only going to be there overnight before being transported to Fürstenfeldbruck the next day. I desperately wanted to see my parents, so I paid one of the German dock workers two packs of cigarettes to go tell my parents that I had arrived. (In the black market economy of post-war Germany, you could buy almost anything with coffee or cigarettes.) He walked several miles to Surheide, the neighborhood where my parents lived on the southeastern outskirts of Bremerhaven, and informed them where I was. Greatly excited at the news, Mom and Dad grabbed their bicycles and rode across town to the harbor area. My mother wasn't allowed to come inside the gate, but my dad had a pass because he was employed near the docks.

When I heard that my dad was there to see me, I ran to him and we fell into each other's arms for a happy reunion after seven long years of separation. Then the two of us walked out to the gate, where I talked to my mother waiting on the other side of the fence. Finally Mom and Dad had to leave, so they reluctantly pedaled away.

The next day I was shipped down to Fürstenfeldbruck. Before and during the war Fürstenfeldbruck had been a base for the German Luftwaffe (Air Force), but was appropriated by the United States at the end of the war for use as an Army Air Corps base.

Germany had been divided by the Allies into three zones of occupation. Bavaria, where I was stationed, was part of the American Zone in the south. Geographically, Bremerhaven was situated inside the northwestern British Zone, but was actually an American Zone enclave within the British Zone. And then there was the eastern Russian Zone, where my uncle Paul Gebhardt and his family now lived in Thuringia. Even though the Russians had been an ally during the war, distrust of their communist government and expansionist intentions had caused relations between them and their former allies to deteriorate. That was the start of the "Cold War" period. Since I had relatives living in the Russian Zone, there was concern that pressure might somehow be put on me through the Russians' treatment of my relatives. That made me a security risk, so I wasn't able to obtain my 320 security clearance to work *officially* as an interpreter.

Instead, I was utilized in the dining hall where about 150 local Germans were employed. I was the assistant mess sergeant, so by default, I was an interpreter anyway, assigning work and translating instructions to the German workers. At one point I was temporarily assigned to work in the Officers' Club, but then was returned to my duties in the dining hall.

In January of 1947 Mabel and Willy finally were able to join me, arriving on the 21st of the month. Willy was ten days short of being seventeen months old.

At Fürstenfeldbruck we lived in a housing development just outside the base which the Army had taken over for its own personnel. There was a sort of yard area for the common use of all the families living there. With cigarettes and coffee as barter for German labor, I had a number of improvements made to this area. I had it fenced and had sandboxes installed for the children, as well as clotheslines where the residents could hang their laundry out to dry. As I mentioned earlier, cigarettes and coffee were the most common currency in dealings with the German population. The war had devastated the German economy, and cash for them was almost nonexistent. With those two items, you could very cheaply buy just about anything you needed in the way of goods and services. They in turn would use the coffee and cigarettes to barter with their fellow Germans. We even had a German maid, which, given the economic conditions, most of the American military families could easily afford.

An Army shuttle bus provided transportation between the housing units and the base or the town. There was a stop right in front of our complex.

On June 28, 1947 a horrible tragedy struck our little family. I was at work in the mess hall that day as usual. Mabel needed to do some shopping at the commissary, so she left Willy in the care of our maid, who put him out in the yard to play in the sandbox. A neighbor's maid came into the yard to hang some clothes on the line, but neglected to close the gate, so Willy wandered out toward the street. About that time the shuttle bus arrived, so one of the neighbor women went out to the bus and he followed without her realizing it.

Willy was twenty-two months old, and just at the age when things like trucks and jeeps and other vehicles were starting to fascinate him. Unnoticed, he wandered around to the front of the bus. Being so small, he was below the bus driver's field of vision, and the driver wasn't even aware he was there. When the bus pulled away, Willy was knocked down. Beneath the bus he apparently tried to scramble to his feet again, but hit his head on the drive train, which dazed him and knocked him to the ground again. At that point the left rear tire of the bus ran over his body. A woman witnessed all of this taking place from the second floor window of her apartment and began yelling to get the driver's attention, but he couldn't hear her and continued on his way.

The ambulance was called and I was notified at work that my little boy had been run over. They told me to go to the hospital to see him. When I arrived at the hospital, Willy was in a crib, and as soon as he saw me he stood up, put his arms around me, and said "Daddy, Daddy!" Relieved that he seemed to be O.K., I decided I should go fetch Mabel at the commissary and bring her back to see him.

When we returned to the hospital they wouldn't let us in to see our little boy, as he had taken a turn for the worse. We were told he was going to be transported by ambulance to the hospital in Munich. They instructed us to go home and change clothes, and then we could follow in a second ambulance.

Distraught as we were, that fifteen-mile trip to Munich was pure torture. To make matters worse, it was a rough and bumpy ride, because the road was full of potholes, still torn up by wartime tank traffic.

Upon arrival at the hospital in Munich, we were devastated to learn that our son had already passed away on the examining table. Our grief was overwhelming, and Mabel was hysterical. "If only they had let me hold him," she cried, "this wouldn't have happened! I could have saved his life!" For months afterward she was inconsolable.

Willy was buried at the International Cemetery in Fürstenfeldbruck, and Mom, Dad and Inge came down from Bremerhaven for the funeral. His burial there was only temporary however, since we planned to have him disinterred and shipped to the United States for reburial when the time came for us to return home.

On September 18, 1947 the Army Air Corps was separated from the Army and became a newly created branch of the military, the United States Air Force. So now I was in the Air Force instead of the Army. At that time I was reassigned to work as interpreter for the German extra gang, which had been hired to do repairs on the railway line that ran between the base and the nearby town of Maisach.

Bavaria's railway system was composed almost exclusively of electrically powered trains, similar to a streetcar. A conventional train with a locomotive had to be turned around when the end of a line was reached in order to travel in the opposite direction. Instead of a locomotive, these electric trains had controls in both the front and rear cars. That way, the engineer could simply relocate to the car on the opposite end and drive away without turning the train around.

One train in particular was composed of two cars that had once been Hitler's personal excursion train. Now it was used by the American military to transport officers around Bavaria. On weekends I was sometimes required to accompany these officers, again serving as interpreter. I got to know quite a few of these officers who were admirable men. Many of them were pilots. The Berlin Airlift started while I was in Germany (June 26, 1948), and some of the pilots I met were probably involved in that. (The Airlift ended in May of 1949, after I had already returned to the States.)

Our daughter, Sonja Joann, was born on May 17, 1948 in the Munich hospital. Even though she was born outside of the United States, she was nevertheless an American citizen by virtue of the fact that one parent (her mother) was a citizen. Shortly thereafter, I was informed that I would be transferred back to the United States by the end of the year. So in June, the casket with our little boy in it was disinterred for shipment to Pekin, Illinois, where Mabel's sister Velda lived. My intention was to try getting stationed at a base near there, but as it turned out, that assignment didn't happen. The marker for Willy's grave was an oval-shaped plaque that I'd had fabricated by a German coppersmith. Yet another thing that was paid for with black market trade goods.

• • •

17

BACK IN THE UNITED STATES

We weren't sent home to the States until November because the Air Force wanted us to allow time for Willy's reburial in Pekin, and not follow immediately.

Before boarding the troop ship in Bremerhaven that would take us home, we visited my parents and sister Inge one last time to say our good-byes and give them the chance to hold five-month-old Sonja in their arms.

During our ocean transit the men and women were berthed in separate areas of the ship, but of course we had our meals together, as well as sharing time otherwise. The sea was rough and Mabel got a little queasy at times, but I don't think she ever got seasick enough to actually vomit. I had been fortunate in that during all the years I had ever spent at sea, I never had a problem with seasickness. This trip was no exception.

When we arrived in New York I had a couple weeks of leave before I was supposed to report on December 15th to Rapid City Air Force Base in South Dakota. Our plan was to take a train to Carrington, North Dakota and visit Mabel's parents. First, however, I took the opportunity to renew old acquaintances there in New York City. Since I had last seen him, my Uncle

John Bolten had moved to a farm near Binghamton, but my cousins were still around, so I at least had a chance to see them. We also visited some of my friends in the Brooklyn area.

After arriving in Carrington we decided that when it came time to leave, I would take the bus to Rapid City and find us a place to live before Mabel and Sonja followed after. Meanwhile, they would remain in Carrington a little longer.

On December 15, 1948 I reported for duty. When I got off the bus in Rapid City, I asked some bystanders where Weaver was. They said, "We don't know, but there's an Air Force base east of town. Maybe Weaver is just part of the address." Well, as it turned out, Weaver was the name the base had very briefly acquired earlier that year, until local protests got it changed back to Rapid City Air Force Base. The name had simply never been corrected on my orders. (In 1953, the name was changed to Ellsworth Air Force Base, which it still is to this day.)

Rapid City is situated in southwestern South Dakota along the eastern foothills of a small, beautiful, forested mountain range called the Black Hills. The east part of town extends out into the Great Plains, but the west side nestles up against the Black Hills. The Air Force Base is about ten miles or so directly east of Rapid City, out in the plains. It's also up on a plateau that's a little higher than the surrounding landscape, which makes it a good place for airplanes to take off and land.

Housing was scarce in Rapid City, but I was able to find a small basement apartment for us to live in.

Mabel and Sonja arrived by bus in Rapid City on New Year's Day, 1949. That was a Saturday. The next day, Sunday, January 2nd, we were hit by the worst blizzard in South Dakota history, before or since. It struck in the morning and didn't let up for four days. Fourteen inches of snow driven by winds up to seventy miles per hour piled up drifts as high as twenty feet in places. The temperature got down as low as four degrees below zero Fahrenheit. The base command told those of us living in town to just stay home. Everything was shut down and nobody could go anywhere anyway. I finally had to dig out at least enough to find someplace I could get some milk for baby Sonja. Quite a monumental task, considering that I had to shovel up from our doorway below ground level through hard-packed snow that had completely buried the steps leading down to it. That storm was quite a dramatic introduction to our life in South Dakota.

A few days after the storm had ended, enough of a one-lane path was finally cleared on the highway to the base which allowed me to get back to work. That blizzard was actually only the first in a series of storms that continued into February. None were quite as severe or as long-lasting as that first one, but they piled more snow on top of what was already on the ground, and recently cleared travel corridors were drifted back in.

When the second blizzard struck on January 15th I was at work on the base and got stranded there. The only somewhat comfortable place we cooks could sleep was in some big rag bins. At the time we still used coal-fired cook stoves, which had to be disassembled every evening and cleaned. That process used up a lot of rags, so we stored the unused clean ones in those bins.

After a few days we ran out of rations, so we were resupplied by air drops from C-47 airplanes flying out of the base at Omaha, Nebraska. They'd fly over and drop coal and C-Rations. These same planes were also pressed into service to drop hay and cotton cake to thousands of starving cattle and other livestock on ranches all over western South Dakota.

Snow had drifted all the way to the roof of the dining hall. Personnel who were still on the base and attempting to reach the dining hall had to form human chains, each holding on to the man in front of him to avoid being blown away and separated. They would trudge up the slope of a drift, move along the length of the building, and when they found the cavity in the snow where the entrance door was located, would slide down to the ground.

When the next blizzard came I was again at work on the base. This time, three of us decided that regardless of the restrictions against leaving the base, we were going home. So we slipped out the gate and set off into the howling wind over the tops of the drifts for the ten or twelve mile trek to Rapid City. En route was a tavern we called Duster's Place, where we often dropped in for a couple of beers after work. (That was before commitment to my Christian faith enabled me to give up drinking alcohol.) So on that day we stopped there for a short rest and just to warm up a bit. We were still

Our kids, Summer 1964: Sonja, Kimalee, Gloria, Richard T.

wearing our white cooks' uniforms, so we changed into the civilian clothes we had brought with us. After thawing out for forty-five minutes or so, we bundled up in our heavy military issue parkas, laced the hoods up tight with only our eyes exposed, and headed out again.

The entire hike from the base to where I lived in town took me about three hours to complete. I was so exhausted when I got home that I fell into bed and slept for the better part of three days. The effort had been worth it though, because otherwise I would have been stuck on the base for a week.

Surprisingly few people lost their lives as a result of the blizzards that winter, but ranchers lost thousands of cattle and sheep. The arrival of spring was a welcome relief.

That summer I became a proud citizen of the United States of America. With eight other new Americans, on July 11, 1949 I swore the oath of allegiance to my country during a naturalization ceremony at the Seventh Judicial Circuit Court in Rapid City. The dream I'd held for twelve long years was finally realized.

As time went on, Sonja acquired three siblings. Our second daughter, Gloria Ellen, was born on December 13, 1949 in the Rapid City hospital. Next was our son, Richard Timothy, born July 2, 1955 in the hospital at Ellsworth Air Force Base. (He has my first name, but he wouldn't be considered a "Junior," since I don't have a middle name.) Finally, there was our youngest daughter, Kimalee Carmen, born October 30, 1962, also at the Ellsworth hospital. When the kids were old enough, Mabel went to work for a number of years as a bookkeeper in the Pennington County Treasurer's office.

Upon completing twenty years of military service I retired from the Air Force on June 30, 1964 with the rank of Staff Sergeant (E-5). For most of my time at Ellsworth I had been in charge of the mess hall. I consider myself fortunate that since first reporting for duty there in 1948, I've never been permanently stationed elsewhere. I did have a temporary one-year assignment to Goose Bay, Labrador (Canada) in 1957, but returned home when that obligation was fulfilled. Mabel and the kids remained behind in Rapid City while I was away. I also once spent several weeks at Maxwell Air Force Base in Montgomery, Alabama for specialized training. But as I said, those were just temporary assignments.

After retirement I supplemented my meager pension by working as head cook at a couple of different nursing homes for the elderly (first at Strathaven Manor and then at Beebe Retirement Home). Eventually I decided to take the Federal Civil Service exam. I passed the exam and was hired to work back in the very same mess hall at Ellsworth where I had been for years, but this time as a civilian employee. I did that for ten years. So with the combination of active military service and Civil Service employment, I ended up having thirty years working for the federal government.

For a brief time we had a little drive-through restaurant called Dick's Drive-In, located directly across Jackson Boulevard from Canyon Lake Park. Mabel and I ran it in alternating shifts, since I was still employed at the air base. Our son Richard T. was a part-time employee when he was in high school, and we also hired a couple of his classmates. Unfortunately, the flash flood of June 9, 1972 not only killed 238 people in Rapid City, but pretty much devastated the surrounding neighborhood that was our main customer base. Business dwindled to almost nothing, so we sold the business property to pay off the loans.

The Rapid City area has been a good place to live and raise our kids. Over the years we bought and lived in three different houses. One was on Omaha Street, another on East Ohio Street in the Robinsdale neighborhood, and the third on Fairway Drive. (Fairway Drive eventually had its name changed to Chapel Lane.) The Black Hills provided opportunities to fish, picnic and camp in some beautiful natural settings. Our Christian faith has been an important part of lives, and we've been active with the Assemblies of God church since shortly after we came here. After they were grown, our kids all eventually left home, got married, and had children of their own. But Mabel and I have lived in Rapid City continuously since that winter of 1948/1949.

I have been blessed.

• • •

trillium memory books

For more information or to order additional copies, please visit:
www.TrilliumMemoryBooks.com

www.ingramcontent.com/pod-product-compliance
Lightning Source LLC
Chambersburg PA
CBHW050614110426
42813CB00008B/2560